Tell Me Why

WHY?

Elephants Have Trunks

Katie Marsico

Published in the United States of America by Cherry Lake Publishing
Ann Arbor, Michigan
www.cherrylakepublishing.com

Content Adviser: Dr. Stephen S. Ditchkoff, Professor of Wildlife Sciences, Auburn University,
Auburn, Alabama
Reading Adviser: Marla Conn, ReadAbility, Inc.

Photo Credits: © PathDoc/Shutterstock Images, cover, 1, 19; © xavier gallego morell/
Shutterstock Images, cover, 1, 11; © michaeljung/Shutterstock Images, cover, 1, 7, back cover;
© jo Crebbin/Shutterstock Images, cover, 1, 11; © michael Sheehan/Shutterstock Images, cover, 1, 17;
© Matt Gibson/Shutterstock Images, cover, 1, 7; © paula French/Shutterstock Images, 5 ; © Sean
Nel/Shutterstock Images, 9; © worradirek/Shutterstock Images, 13; © Jez Bennett/Shutterstock
Images, 15; © Blaine Stuart/Shutterstock Images, 19; © CapPui/Shuttterstock Images, 21

Library of Congress Cataloging-in-Publication Data

Marsico, Katie, 1980- author.
  Elephants have trunks / by Katie Marsico.
     pages cm. -- (Tell me why)
  Summary: "Offers answers to the most compelling questions about this large
animal that uses its trunk to eat and drink. Age-appropriate explanations
and appealing photos. Additional text features and search tools help
students locate information and learn new words"-- Provided by publisher.
  Audience: Grade K to 3.
  Includes bibliographical references and index.
  ISBN 978-1-63188-002-5 (hardcover) -- ISBN 978-1-63188-045-2 (pbk.) --
ISBN 978-1-63188-088-9 (pdf) -- ISBN 978-1-63188-131-2 (ebook) 1.
Elephants--Juvenile literature. 2. Children's questions and answers. I.
Title.

QL795.E4M28 2015
599.67--dc23
                              2014005728

Cherry Lake Publishing would like to acknowledge the work of The Partnership for 21st Century
Skills. Please visit www.p21.org for more information.

Printed in the United States of America
Corporate Graphics Inc.
July 2014

Table of Contents

Body Part or Broken Vacuum

Achoo! Gino is suddenly surrounded by dust at the zoo. He just saw an elephant use its **trunk** to suck up a pile of dirt. It reminded Gino of his parents' vacuum. Yet, unlike their vacuum, the animal blew the dust back out again. Gino wonders why elephants have a trunk. All he knows is that it's good for making a mess.

Elephants sometimes shower themselves with dirt to protect their skin.

Elephants are the largest land mammals on Earth. Mammals are **warm-blooded** animals that produce milk to feed their babies. They are usually covered in hair or fur. Elephants don't look furry. But they have thin, wiry hairs on their head and back.

Some elephants weigh up to 8 tons (7,257 kilograms)! That's about the same weight as three to four sport-utility vehicles. These huge mammals measure 18 to 24 feet (5.5 to 7.3 meters) long.

This is an elephant's trunk. Is the elephant's skin smooth or rough? What do you notice about the tip, or end, of the trunk?

An elephant's trunk is very flexible.

7

Elephants live in different **habitats** in Africa and Asia. Some are found in **rain forests**. Others spend most of their time in dry, grassy plains.

Elephants are herbivores. An herbivore is an animal that only feeds on plant matter. An elephant's diet is mainly made up of grasses, leaves, bamboo, bark, and roots. Adults sometimes eat 300 to 400 pounds (136 to 181 kg) of food every day.

Elephants use their trunks to suck up water.
Then they spray the water into their open mouths.

Not Just a Nose

Gino watches the elephant scoop up hay and fruit with its trunk. Maybe it's more than a messy vacuum after all. The **zookeeper** tells Gino that elephants use their trunk the same way people use their hands.

She explains that the trunk is a prehensile body part. This means that elephants are able to grasp and hold objects with it. They also rely on their trunk to touch, reach, pick up, push, pull, and even throw things.

MAKE A GUESS!

What if elephants had bones in their trunk instead of muscle? Would it change how elephants are able to use their trunks?

An elephant uses its trunk to lift food to it's mouth.

11

An elephant's trunk measures up to 6.5 feet (2 m) long. It often weighs as much as 440 pounds (200 kg). The trunk is both a nose and upper lip that contains 150,000 pieces of muscle.

At its tip are a pair of **nostrils** and one to two fingerlike points. The nostrils are used for smelling and breathing. The fingerlike growths are what allow elephants to grab and hold objects.

An elephant relies on its trunk to pick up and hold many different objects.

From Grabbing to Greeting

The zookeeper tells Gino that elephants' ancestors, or early relatives, had a shorter trunk. Yet it grew longer and stronger as elephants **adapted** to the world around them. Today, they use their trunk to get food and water from areas that other animals often find hard to reach. Elephants are able to grab leaves and branches high up in the treetops. They also rely on their trunk to dig up dirt and rocks that cover underground streams.

Having a trunk allows elephants to reach high into the treetops!

Elephants also spray water, dust, and grass out their trunk and onto their body. This protects them from the hot rays of the sun.

Elephants depend on their trunk to **communicate**, too. They move it into different positions to greet each other, show affection, and even fight. Sometimes elephants communicate by making noises with their trunk. They create many sounds —including trumpet calls—by forcing air out their nostrils.

Elephants use their trunks to communicate.

A Lot More to Learn

Gino is amazed by everything he's learned. He still has a few questions though. He wonders if an elephant would be able to lift him with its trunk. The zookeeper says yes!

Elephants have been known to raise objects weighing as much as 660 pounds (300 kg) with their trunk. This prehensile body part is strong enough to knock over a tree. Yet an elephant's trunk is also **agile** enough to pick up something as tiny as a peanut.

What if an elephant needs to swim across a river? Would its trunk come in handy? Go online with an adult or visit your library to find the answer.

The trunk is an extremely powerful body part.

Gino wants to find out more about elephants and their terrific trunk. The zookeeper says it's important for people to get to know these amazing animals. She explains that some elephants are **endangered**. Everyone needs to do their part to help protect them. Gino decides to share what he's learned with his teachers, friends, and family. He loved visiting the elephants—even if he got a little dusty doing it.

People can learn more about elephants at zoos
and wildlife centers.

Think About It

Do other animals have a prehensile body part? See if you can name another mammal with a prehensile part. How about a fish?

Are Asian elephants different from African elephants? Find another book about elephants. Use it to make a list of the similarities and differences.

Some elephants are endangered. Go online with an adult or visit your library to learn how people are trying to save elephants.

Glossary

adapted (uh-DAHP-tuhd) changed to fit the needs of a new situation or environment

agile (AH-juhl) able to move with speed and grace

communicate (kuh-MYOO-nuh-kayte) to share thoughts, feelings, or other information

endangered (in-DAYNE-juhrd) in danger of completely dying out

habitats (HA-buh-tats) the places where plants and animals normally live and grow

nostrils (NAHS-truhlz) openings on the nose that are used for smelling and breathing

rain forests (RAYNE FOR-uhstz) tropical forests that feature tall trees and a large amount of rainfall

trunk (TRUHNK) a long, muscular body part that is both a nose and an upper lip

warm-blooded (WARM-BLUH-duhd) having a body temperature that doesn't change because of outside temperature changes

zookeeper (ZOO-kee-pur) a person in charge of a zoo's animals

Find Out More

Books:

Brennan, Francis. *Elephants.* New York: Children's Press, 2013.

Hanson, Anders. *Elephant.* Minneapolis: ABDO Publishing Company, 2014.

Lindeen, Mary. *Elephants.* Minneapolis: Jump! 2014.

Web Sites:

National Geographic Kids—African Elephants
www.kids.nationalgeographic.com/kids/animals/creaturefeature/african-elephant
Check out this Web site for more fast facts on African elephants, as well as photos, a video, a sound clip, and an e-card.

San Diego Zoo Kids—African Elephants
http://kids.sandiegozoo.org/animals/mammals/african-elephant
This Web page contains photos, further information, and a webcam that displays real-time footage of the zoo's elephants.

Index

About the Author

Katie Marsico is the author of more than 150 children's books. She lives in a suburb of Chicago, Illinois, with her husband and children.